D1267067

SUPER
SANDCASTLE
It's the Alphabet!

It's K!

Kelly Doudna

Consulting Editor, Diane Craig, M.A./Reading Specialist

ABDO
Publishing Company

Published by ABDO Publishing Company, 8000 West 78th Street, Edina, Minnesota 55439. Copyright © 2010 by Abdo Consulting Group, Inc. International copyrights reserved in all countries. No part of this book may be reproduced in any form without written permission from the publisher. Super SandCastle™ is a trademark and logo of ABDO Publishing Company.

Printed in the United States.

♻ PRINTED ON RECYCLED PAPER

Editor: Katherine Hengel
Content Developer: Nancy Tuminelly
Cover and Interior Design and Production: Kelly Doudna, Mighty Media
Photo Credits: iStockphoto (Jani Bryson), Shutterstock

Library of Congress Cataloging-in-Publication Data
Doudna, Kelly, 1963-
  It's K! / Kelly Doudna.
    p. cm. -- (It's the Alphabet!)
  ISBN 978-1-60453-598-3
  1. English language--Alphabet--Juvenile literature. 2. Alphabet books--Juvenile literature. I. Title.
  PE1155.D684 2010
  421'.1--dc22
  〈E〉
                          2009021008

Super SandCastle™ books are created by a team of professional educators, reading specialists, and content developers around five essential components— phonemic awareness, phonics, vocabulary, text comprehension, and fluency—to assist young readers as they develop reading skills and strategies and increase their general knowledge. All books are written, reviewed, and leveled for guided reading, early reading intervention, and Accelerated Reader® programs for use in shared, guided, and independent reading and writing activities to support a balanced approach to literacy instruction.

About SUPER SANDCASTLE™

Bigger Books for Emerging Readers Grades K–4

Created for library, classroom, and at-home use, Super SandCastle™ books support and engage young readers as they develop and build literacy skills and will increase their general knowledge about the world around them. Super SandCastle™ books are an extension of SandCastle™, the leading preK–3 imprint for emerging and beginning readers. Super SandCastle™ features a larger trim size for more reading fun.

Let Us Know
Super SandCastle™ would like to hear your stories about reading this book. What was your favorite page? Was there something hard that you needed help with? Share the ups and downs of learning to read. We want to hear from you! Send us an e-mail.

sandcastle@abdopublishing.com

Contact us for a complete list of SandCastle™, Super SandCastle™, and other nonfiction and fiction titles from ABDO Publishing Company.

www.abdopublishing.com • 8000 West 78th Street
Edina, MN 55439 • 800-800-1312 • 952-831-1632 fax

Aa Bb Cc Dd Ee
Ff Gg Hh Ii Jj Kk
Ll Mm Nn Oo Pp
Qq Rr Ss Tt Uu Vv
Ww Xx Yy Zz

The Letter Kk

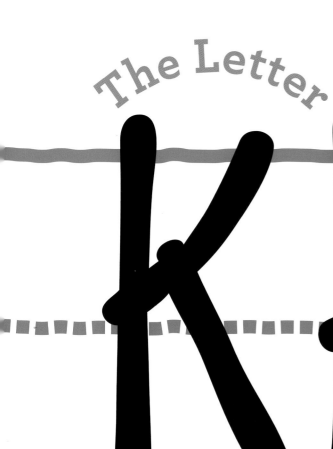

The letter k in American Sign Language

K and k can also look like

Kk **Kk** Kk Kk Kk Kk

The letter k is
a consonant.

It is the 11th
letter of the
alphabet.

☞ Some words start with **k**.

kangaroo

koala

Katie keeps a koala and a kangaroo in the kitchen.

Katie

7

Some words have **k** in the middle.

basket

blanket

cookie

8

Brooklyn

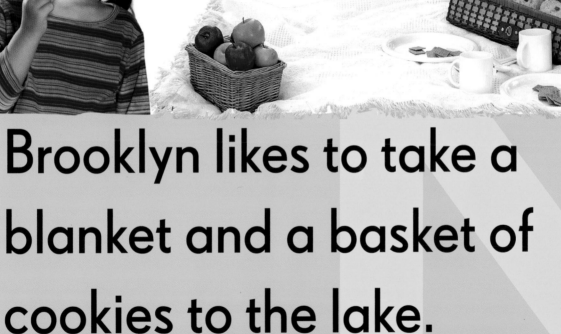

Brooklyn likes to take a blanket and a basket of cookies to the lake.

lake

9

Some words have **k** at the end.

elk

oak

10

Hi, Mark!

On his walk in the park, Mark saw a pink oak and an elk that could talk.

truck

Jackson snacks on pickles in the back of his black truck.

pickle

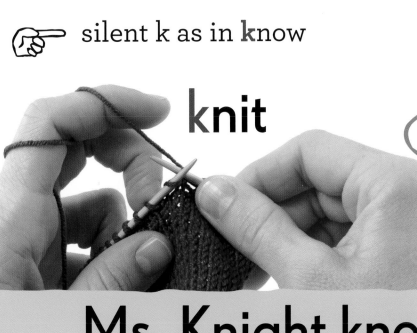

silent k as in **k**now

knit

A silent k always has the letter n after it.

Ms. Knight knows how to knit knickers that cover her knees.

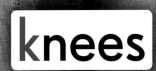

knees

13

14

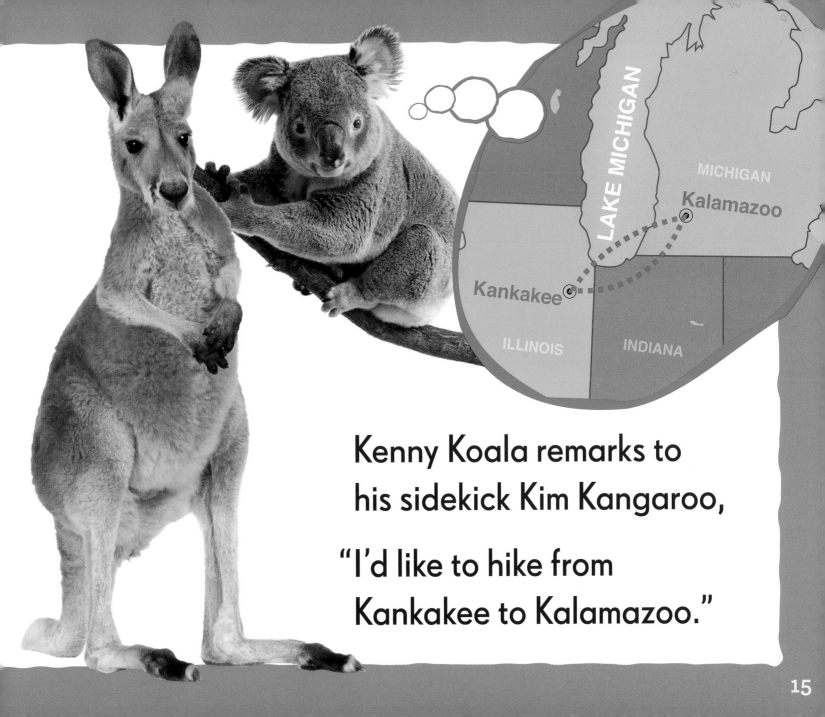

Kenny Koala remarks to his sidekick Kim Kangaroo,

"I'd like to hike from Kankakee to Kalamazoo."

They pack cornflakes for breakfast and cupcakes for snacks.

They stick all of their junk in black and khaki backpacks.

They get to Lake Michigan
and know it's too far to walk.

They kick off their shoes and
take a quick break to talk.

Kenny says, "Let's make a new plan and cross the lake in a kayak."

Kim says, "Then we'll pick up some bikes for our journey back."

They kayak across Lake Michigan and make it to Kalamazoo.

They bike back to Kankakee and think, "That was fun to do!"

Kenny and Kim think of
a new trek and feel pretty lucky.

They'll take a pickup truck
to see Chuck in Kentucky.

MICHIGAN

Kalamazoo

ANA

OHIO

KENTUCKY

Kentucky

Which words have
the letter **k**?

ladybug

kayak

bird

bike

koala

train

truck

basket

Glossary

backpack (p. 16) – a bag you wear on your back.

hike (p. 15) – to take a long walk, especially in the country.

journey (p. 18) – a trip or vacation.

kayak (pp. 18, 19, 22) – 1. a small, narrow boat that you sit in and move with a paddle. 2. to paddle a kayak.

khaki (p. 16) – a yellowish brown color.

knickers (p. 13) – loose pants that end just below the knee.

knit (p. 13) – to connect loops of yarn or thread using needles.

pickup (p. 20) – a small truck with an open bed.

remark (p. 15) – to say something.

sidekick (p. 15) – a friend, partner, or helper.

trek (p. 20) – a long, slow journey.

To promote letter recognition, letters are highlighted instead of glossary words in this series. The page numbers above indicate where the glossary words can be found.

More Words with **K**

Find the **k** in the beginning, middle, or end of each word.

ask	keg	king	knew	sick
book	key	kiss	knife	skunk
chicken	keyboard	kit	look	sky
donkey	kid	kite	pumpkin	sticky
duck	kin	kitten	quack	thank
keeper	kind	kneel	rock	work